Encounter with the Self

Marie-Louise von Franz, Honorary Patron

**Studies in Jungian Psychology
by Jungian Analysts**

Daryl Sharp, General Editor

Encounter with the Self

A Jungian Commentary
on William Blake's
Illustrations of the Book of Job

Edward F. Edinger

Canadian Cataloguing in Publication Data

Edinger, Edward F. (Edward Ferdinand), 1922-
  Encounter with the self: a Jungian commentary on
William Blake's Illustrations of the book of Job

(Studies in Jungian psychology by Jungian analysts; 22)

Includes bibliographical references.

ISBN 0-919123-21-X

1. Blake, William, 1757-1827.   Illustrations of the
book of Job.   2. Bible.   O. T. Job - Illustrations.
3. Self-actualization (Psychology).   4. God.
5. Jung, C.G. (Carl Gustav), 1875-1961.   I. Blake,
William, 1757-1827.   Illustrations of the book of Job.
II. Title.   III. Series.

NE642.B5E45 1986   769.92'4   C85-090865-5

INNER CITY BOOKS
Box 1271, Station Q, Toronto, Canada M4T 2P4
Telephone (416) 927-0355

Honorary Patron: Marie-Louise von Franz.
Publisher and General Editor: Daryl Sharp.
Editorial Board: Fraser Boa, Daryl Sharp, Marion Woodman.

INNER CITY BOOKS was founded in 1980 to promote the
understanding and practical application of the work of C.G. Jung.

Cover: "When the Morning Stars Sang Together"—William Blake.
(Pierpont Morgan Library, New York)

Printed and bound in Canada by Webcom Limited

CONTENTS

See final pages for descriptions of other Inner City Books

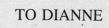

TO DIANNE

Note

The term "Self" is used by Jung to designate the transpersonal center and totality of the psyche. It constitutes the greater, objective personality, whereas the ego is the lesser, subjective personality. Empirically the Self cannot be distinguished from the God-image. Encounter with it is a *mysterium tremendum*.

Preface

The experience of the Self is always a defeat for the ego.
—C.G. Jung, *Mysterium Coniunctionis.*

There is in the unconscious a transpersonal center of latent conscious-ness and obscure intentionality. The discovery of this center, which Jung called the Self, is like the discovery of extraterrestrial intelli-gence. Man is now no longer alone in the psyche and in the cosmos. The vicissitudes of life take on new and enlarged meaning. Dreams, fantasies, illness, accident and coincidence become potential mes-sages from the unseen Partner with whom we share our life.

At first, the encounter with the Self is indeed a defeat for the ego; but with perseverence, *Deo volente,* light is born from the darkness. One meets the ''Immortal One'' who wounds and heals, who casts down and raises up, who makes small and makes large—in a word, the One who makes one *whole*.

Introduction

C.G. Jung's *Answer to Job* has established the story of Job as crucial to the psyche of modern man. With our attention focused on this theme we can now see more clearly the relevance of its other expressions in modern times, as for instance Goethe's *Faust,* Melville's *Moby-Dick* and Blake's *Illustrations of the Book of Job.*

Jung tells us that "the Book of Job serves as a paradigm for a certain experience of God which has a special significance for us today."[1] In other words, the Job story is an archetypal image which pictures a certain typical encounter between the ego and the Self. This typical encounter may be called the Job archetype. The chief features of the Job archetype are: 1) an encounter between the ego and the Greater Personality (God, Angel, Superior being); 2) a wound or suffering of the ego as a result of the encounter; 3) the perseverance of the ego which endures the ordeal and persists in scrutinizing the experience in search of its meaning; and 4) a divine revelation by which the ego is rewarded with some insight into the transpersonal psyche. In addition to the Book of Job there are many other examples of this archetype. For instance, I would mention the following: Jacob and the Angel of Yahweh, Arjuna and Krishna, Paul and Christ, Moses and El-Khidr, Faust and Mephistopheles, Captain Ahab and Moby-Dick, Nietzsche and Zarathustra, Jung and Philemon.

The Book of Job represents an individual ego's decisive encounter with the Self, the Greater Personality. The ego is wounded by this encounter which provokes a descent into the unconscious, a *nekyia.* Because Job perseveres in questioning the meaning of the experience his endurance is rewarded by a divine revelation. The ego, by holding fast to its integrity, is granted a realization of the Self.

1. Jung, *Answer to Job,* in *Psychology and Religion: West and East,* CW 11, par. 562 [CW refers throughout to *The Collected Works of C.G. Jung* (Bollingen Series XX) trans. R.F.C. Hull, ed. H. Read, M. Fordham, G. Adler, Wm. McGuire (Princeton: Princeton University Press, 1953-1979). *Answer to Job* is also available separately (Princeton: Princeton University Press, 1973).]

As a framework for the discussion I have chosen to comment on William Blake's *Illustrations of the Book of Job,* published in 1825. This series of twenty-two engravings is Blake's masterwork, done when he was beyond the age of sixty-five. It was his last major completed work. These engravings are inspired and are worthy to be set beside the story which they illustrate. Blake's rendering of the Job story shows us the effect of this archetypal image on the unconscious of a modern, or almost modern, man. Scholars can inform us what Blake consciously intended to convey in these pictures.[2] However, as with most great works of art, Blake expressed far more than he knew. In these pictures the objective psyche speaks directly to us.

Jung distinguishes between two types of artistic creation, the psychological and the visionary. About the latter he writes,

> It is a primordial experience which surpasses man's understanding and to which in his weakness he may easily succumb. The very enormity of the experience gives it its value and its shattering impact. Sublime, pregnant with meaning, yet chilling the blood with its strangeness, it arises from timeless depths. . . . [In contrast, the psychological mode of artistic creation deals with] experiences of the foreground of life. These never rend the curtain that veils the cosmos; they do not exceed the bounds of our human capacities. . . . But the primordial experiences rend from top to bottom the curtain upon which is painted the picture of an ordered world, and allow a glimpse into the unfathomable abyss of the unborn and of things yet to be. . . .
>
> We find such a vision in the *Shepherd of Hermas,* in Dante, in the second part of *Faust,* in Nietzsche's Dionysian experience, in Wagner's *Ring, Tristan, Parsifal,* in Spitteler's *Olympian Spring,* in William Blake's paintings and poetry, [etc.].[3]

Such a primordial experience as Jung speaks of lies behind these engravings for the Book of Job.

---

2. See, for instance, S. Foster Damon, *Blake's Job* (New York: E.P. Dutton & Co., 1969).
3. Jung, "Psychology and Literature," *The Spirit in Man, Art, and Literature,* CW 15, pars. 141f.

William Blake's

Illustrations of the Book of Job

ספר איוב

ILLUSTRATIONS of

The
BOOK
of
JOB

Invented & Engraved
by William Blake
1825

London Published as the Act directs March 8:1825 by William Blake N°3 Fountain Court Strand

Title Page

Seven winged angels move clockwise from upper right downward and upward to the left. S. Foster Damon informs us that Blake identified these with the seven eyes of God mentioned in Zechariah 4:10 and with the seven eyes of the lamb in Revelation 5:6.[4] According to Jung, Satan, who instigated the whole Job drama, "is presumably one of God's eyes which 'go to and fro in the earth and walk up and down in it' (Job 1:7)."[5] Thus the theme of the "eye of God" is immediately introduced. It is Yahweh's intention, via the machinations of Satan, to *scrutinize* Job. As the drama unfolds, however, the subject and object of scrutiny become reversed.[6]

4. Damon, *Blake's Job,* p. 4.
5. Jung, *Answer to Job,* par. 579, note 3.
6. For more on the "eye of God" theme, see Edward F. Edinger, *The Creation of Consciousness* (Toronto: Inner City Books, 1984), pp. 42ff.

Our Father which art in Heaven   hallowed be thy Name

Thus did Job continually

There was a Man in the
Land of Uz whose Name
was Job. & that Man
was perfect & upright

The Letter Killeth
The Spirit giveth Life

It is Spiritually Discerned

& one that feared God
& eschewed Evil. & there
was born unto him Seven
Sons & Three Daughters

W Blake inv & sculp

London. Published as the Act directs. March 8:1828. by Will Blake N.º Fountain Court Strand.

Picture 1

This picture shows Job's initial state of prosperity and contentment. He and his family are gathered under the tree of life in a state of prayer. It is to be noted that the animals are asleep and the musical instruments are hanging on the tree. A state of innocence and somnolence prevails. Both instinctual and spiritual-cultural energies are not functioning. Job is living "by the book," as suggested by the open books in the laps of both Job and his wife. He is backed up by institutional religion, signified by the cathedral on one side, and his material well-being indicated by the flocks and barns on the other side. But the sun is setting and the moon is in its last phase.

This shows the initial innocent state of the ego that feels secure in its unconscious assumptions and collective containments. It is a state of *participation mystique* with surroundings and social groupings—family, community, church, etc. Above the picture are the first lines of the Lord's prayer, "Our Father which art in Heaven, hallowed be thy name," which suggest that it is an innocent, trusting, "Lord's-prayer" attitude toward God which is about to be sacrificed. The theme of sacrifice is indicated by the altar with the sacrificial fire at the bottom of the picture.

The whole engraving of Job and his family is contained within a cloud of smoke rising from the altar, as though Job were the sacrificial victim. Inscribed on the altar are the words, "The Letter Killeth, The Spirit giveth Life," indicating that it is the word and Job's reliance on it which are to be sacrificed. A tentlike form also frames the picture, as though we were seeing into the tabernacle tent which houses Yahweh's presence. The vast flocks of sheep emphasize the theme of sheeplike docility, collectivity and innocence.

I beheld the Ancient of Days

I shall see God

Hast thou considered my Servant Job

The Angel of the Divine Presence

מלך יהוה

We shall awake up

Thou art our Father

in thy Likeness

When the Almighty was yet with me. When my Children
were about me

There was a day when the Sons of God came to present themselves before the Lord & Satan came also among them
to present himself before the Lord

London Published as the Act directs March 8.1825 by Will Blake N 3 Fountain Court Strand

Proof

Picture 2

In the lower part of the picture, Job seems to be reading and proclaiming the word of the book. Up above in heaven something else is going on. The unconscious has been activated. Yahweh, like Job, has a book in his lap, as though he too had been functioning "by the book." Also many of the angels have books or scrolls. But now an intense dynamism approaches Yahweh. Satan, the autonomous spirit, manifests in a stream of fire. As the urge to individuation and greater consciousness he stirs up doubts and questions which challenge the status quo and destroy the complacent living by the book.

Yahweh and Satan plot to put Job to the test. The question is: Will Job remain loyal to Yahweh in spite of adversity? It is as though Job has known only the benevolent aspects of Yahweh and Yahweh needs to be known in his totality—good and bad. Throughout the Old Testament Yahweh is exceedingly concerned with receiving praise and exclusive recognition from man. Concerning this aspect of Yahweh Jung writes,

> The character thus revealed fits a personality who can only convince himself that he exists through his relation to an object. Such dependence on the object is absolute when the subject is totally lacking in self-reflection and therefore has no insight into himself. It is as if he existed only by reason of the fact that he has an object which assures him that he is really there.[7]

Hence we can hypothesize that it is the Self's need to be known in its totality—its oppositeness—by the ego that initiates the drama of Job.

Blake pictures Satan in terms of intense energy. He is in a cloud of flame and his movements are wild and flamelike. Dionysian energy of excess has erupted into the Apollonian realm of order, measure and form. This picture is reminiscent of a passage in Blake's *The Marriage of Heaven and Hell:*

7. Jung, *Answer to Job,* par. 574.

Without Contraries is no progression. Attraction and Repulsion, Reason and Energy, Love and Hate, are necessary to Human existence.

From these contraries spring what the religious call Good & Evil. Good is the passive that obeys Reason. Evil is the active springing from Energy.

Good is Heaven, Evil is Hell. . . .

*

. . . Those who restrain desire, do so because theirs is weak enough to be restrained; and the restrainer or reason usurps its place & governs the unwilling.

And being restrain'd, it by degrees becomes passive, till it is only the shadow of desire.

The history of this is written in Paradise Lost, & the Governor or Reason is call'd Messiah.

And the original Archangel or possessor of the command of the heavenly host, is call'd the Devil or Satan, and his children are call'd Sin & Death.

But in the Book of Job, Milton's Messiah is call'd Satan.

For this history has been adopted by both parties.

It indeed appear'd to Reason as if Desire was cast out, but the Devil's account is, that the Messiah fell, & formed a heaven of what he stole from the Abyss.

This is shewn in the Gospel, where he prays to the Father to send the comforter, or Desire, that Reason may have Ideas to build on; the Jehovah of the Bible being no other than he who dwells in flaming fire.[8]

If this isn't clear it is because Blake is presenting a paradox. By one account Satan or Desire is evil and to be banished. By another account Satan or Desire is the Messiah who descends to earth for man's salvation. The connection between Blake's fiery Satan and Messiah is also suggested by the uncanonical saying of Jesus, "He who is near to me is close to the fire."[9] In this picture Satan

8. *The Poetry and Prose of William Blake,* ed. David Erdman (Garden City, N.Y.: Anchor Books, 1979), pp. 34f.
9. "The Gospel of Thomas," *The Nag Hammadi Library,* ed. James M. Robinson (San Francisco: Harper & Row, 1977), p. 127.

represents the return of banished energy and desire, which by rejuvenating the personality may function as savior in spite of its apparently destructive effect.

The Fire of God is fallen from Heaven

And the Lord said unto Satan Behold All that he hath is in thy Power

Thy Sons & thy Daughters were eating & drinking Wine in their
eldest Brothers house &: behold there came a great wind from the Wilderness
& smote upon the four faces of the house & it fell upon the young Men & they are Dead

W Blake inv & sculp

London, Published as the Act directs March 8 1825 by W Blake, N 3 Fountain Court Strand

Proof

Picture 3

In this picture the energy dynamism reaches its highest pitch. Almost pure explosive energy erupts into consciousness, destroying its containing structures. The picture shows the destruction of Job's children and their families. Job himself has not yet been touched. For him the effects are still peripheral.

Psychologically, this might correspond to the onset of bad dreams and neurotic symptoms in an individual—anxiety, depression, insomnia and psychosomatic symptoms of all kinds. Dreams of atomic explosions, fires, floods and catastrophes would correspond to this phase of the Job drama.

And there came a Messenger unto Job & said. The Oxen were plowing & the Sabeans came down & they have slain the Young Men with the Sword

Going to & fro in the Earth

& walking up & down in it

And I only am escaped alone to tell thee.

While he was yet speaking
there came also another & said

The fire of God is fallen from heaven & hath burned up the flocks & the
Young Men & consumed them. & I only am escaped alone to tell thee

WBlake invent & sculp

London, Published as the Act directs March 8, 1825 by Will Blake N° 3 Fountain Court Strand

Proof

Picture 4

This picture shows the arrival of the bad news. Three messengers are visible at different distances. In the direction from which they come can be seen a cathedral. This suggests that it is the established religious structure, the traditional container of transpersonal values, that is being destroyed by the energy erupting from the unconscious.

Certainly that was true for Job. Although his so-called comforters counseled him to accept the traditional religious view, Job insisted on being true to his experience though it ran counter to tradition. Likewise in Blake's time, the age of the Enlightenment, the traditional Christian world-view was in the process of being destroyed by the erupting energies of reason, science, materialism and technology. In our picture the fading cathedral in the distance is overshadowed by prominent megalithic Druidic forms in the foreground. There is thus a movement toward more primitive and less differentiated religious structures. This corresponds to the fact that an encounter with the unconscious does tend to break up merely formal, habitual religious patterns and promotes a more vital, albeit more primitive, living connection with transpersonal realities.

As the messengers arrive, Job and his wife look apprehensive. The symptoms of the activated unconscious are reaching awareness and the ego is alarmed.

5

Did I not weep for him who was in trouble? Was not my Soul afflicted for the Poor?

Behold he is in thy hand; but save his Life

Then went Satan forth from the presence of the Lord

And it grieved him at his heart

Who maketh his Angels Spirits & his Ministers a Flaming Fire

WBlake inventor & sculp

London, Published as the Act directs March 8 1825, by Will. Blake N.º 3 Fountain Court Strand

Proof

Job has reacted to his symptoms by an intensified emphasis on the conventional virtues. He is shown here distributing alms, while in heaven Satan is about to pour fire on him. Yahweh on his throne looks as despondent as Job. Both have fallen into a neurasthenic state while Satan is in command of immense energies. Job's losses— servants, flocks and family—have fallen into the unconscious. The energies that have been lost to the conscious personality have increased the energy charge of the unconscious.

This picture shows the way the ego often tries at first to deal with psychic symptoms. Rather than confront them and learn their meaning, it splits them off and dissociates them from consciousness. The net result is an impoverishment of the conscious personality, which can continue to function only with minimal energy and under severe limitations. The dissociated state is indicated by the sharp line of demarcation which separates the human world from the divine world.

Naked came I out of my mothers womb & Naked shall I return thither

The Lord gave & the Lord hath taken away. Blessed be the Name of the Lord

And smote Job with sore Boils
from the sole of his foot to the crown of his head

W Blake inv & sc

London, as Act directs Published March 8: 1825 by William Blake N.º 3 Fountain Court Strand

Proof

Picture 6

Here even the limited adaptation breaks down. The activated unconscious now pours itself directly on to Job, the ego.

This is the picture of an acute breakdown; all defenses have collapsed. The picture shows Job being stricken with boils. In dreams boils represent festering, neglected complexes which are erupting into consciousness. If the urgent needs of the unconscious have been neglected they are then apt to take on a negative, pathological aspect and force the ego to give them attention by inflicting pain. This is the last glimpse of the sun. It will not reappear until the final picture.

Satan has four arrows in his right hand with which he is about to pierce Job. This means that Job is being attacked by the quaternity, the wholeness of the Self. He is to be transfixed, pinned to the earth, as in certain alchemical pictures which show this happening to Mercurius. In alchemy this is an image of *coagulatio* (a process

Mercurius pinned to a tree, from "Speculum veritatis"
(MS., 17th cent.)

29

The Ecstasy of St. Theresa, sculpture by Bernini

of solidification or concretization)[10] and is analogous to Christ's being nailed to the cross. One may also think of Cupid's arrow of passion and of Bernini's sculpture, *The Ecstasy of St. Theresa.*

The broken pitcher below the picture suggests that the ego as a container may break if more is poured into it than it can stand. The motif of the broken vessel is found in the Lurianic Cabbala.[11] According to this doctrine the creation of the finite world required that the divine light be poured into bowls or vessels. Some of these bowls (the seven lower Sefiroth of the Sefirotic tree) could not stand the impact of the light and broke, causing the light to spill. This picture suggests that Job is such a vessel. Like the Apostle Paul, Job could be called a chosen vessel to bear God's name.[12] Job in fact did not break. His ego remained intact. He maintained his integrity and thus served as a vessel for the divine consciousness. The broken shepherd's crook in the lower left corner indicates the loss of an innocent, "The-Lord-is-my-shepherd" attitude. Certainly what is happening to Job in this picture, with Yahweh's permission, does not square with the idea of Yahweh as a good shepherd. It reminds us of Yahweh's words and actions as expressed through his prophet Zechariah:

> No longer am I going to show kindness to the inhabitants of the world—it is Yahweh who speaks. But instead I mean to hand over every man to the next, and to his king. They shall devastate the world and I will not deliver them from their hands. Then I began to pasture these sheep bred for slaughter for the sheep dealers. I took two staves: one I called Goodwill, the other Union. And so I began to pasture the sheep. . . . But I began to dislike the sheep and they equally detested me. I then said, "I am going to pasture you no longer; let those that wish to die, die; let those that wish to perish, perish; and let those that are left devour each other's flesh!" I then took my staff, Goodwill, and broke it in half, to break my covenant that I had made with all the peoples.[13]

10. See Edward F. Edinger, *Anatomy of the Psyche* (La Salle, IL: Open Court, 1985), chapter 4.
11. See Gershom Scholem, *Major Trends in Jewish Mysticism* (New York: Schocken Books, 1954), p. 266.
12. Acts 9:15.
13. Zechariah 11:6-10; Jerusalem Bible.

In this passage God pours out his wrath on mankind; that is, primitive rage from the unconscious pours into the conscious personality, generating wars and murderous dissension.

This picture shows Job being afflicted with disease. It reminds us that illness as subjectively experienced is a divine manifestation that "crosses our willful path."[14] Whatever its more specific message may be, a painful disease or injury demands that the ego give *attention* to the non-ego. Pain is the great enigma of existence. It is the perpetual dark companion to sentient being. A patient in the aftermath of an experience of intense pain (renal colic) found these words forming themselves within him:

Going to School to Pain

Pain says: If one would teach, he must first get the student's attention. I am an excellent attention-getter.

I am deep. If you would not fear me, be deep like me.

I come from the center. A point is my sign. A stab from me is the Cosmic Goad.

If you would not fear me, live each Present Moment with the same intensity that you experience me.

I am the great purifier. Only the essential can endure me. All else is burnt away.

I am the great valuer. All values come from me and my partner, Death.

I am the gateway to the Mysteries. An image of me is your highest concept of the Sacred. I am the quintessential Now. I lie in ambush for those who miss their daily dose of life. This elixir, unconsumed, accumulates and overspills its little vial, raining its concentrated torrent on the negligent soul.

I am the angel of Annunciation for the awesome Now. Time is a gliding serpent bearing precious jewels upon its back—each jewel a Present Moment.

14. Jung is quoted as saying, "God is the name by which I designate all things which cross my willful path violently and recklessly, all things which upset my subjective views, plans and intentions and change the course of my life for better or worse." Interview in *Good Housekeeping Magazine,* December 1961.

What! shall we recieve Good
at the hand of God & shall we not also
recieve Evil

And when they lifted up their eyes afar off & knew him not
they lifted up their voice & wept. & they rent every Man his
mantle & sprinkled dust upon their heads towards heaven

Ye have heard of the Patience of Job and have seen the end of the Lord.

W Blake inven & sculpt

London. Published as the Act directs March 8.1825 by William Blake N.3 Fountain Court Strand

Proof

Picture 7

This picture shows the arrival of Job's "comforters"—Eliphaz, Bildad and Zophar. These three represent shadow figures who are brought into conscious view with the breakdown of the ego. As Job loses the defensive boundaries of his conscious personality, repressed aspects of himself come into view. They at first do not speak. Job, the ego, first bewails his fate in the next picture.

Lo let that night be solitary
& let no joyful voice come therein

Let the Day perish wherein I was Born

And they sat down with him upon the ground seven days & seven
nights & none spake a word unto him for they saw that his grief
was very great

London. Published as the Act directs March 8: 1825 by Will Blake N 3 Fountain Court Strand

Picture 8

Job now succumbs to the *nigredo,* the dark night of the soul. He falls into blackness and suicidal despair.

> May the day perish when I was born,
> and the night that told of a boy conceived,
> May that day be darkness.
> May God on high have no thought for it,
> May no light shine on it.
> . . . .
> Why did I not die new-born,
> not perish as I left the womb?
> Why were there two knees to receive me,
>   two breasts for me to suck?
> Had there not been, I should now be lying in peace,
>   wrapped in a restful slumber,
> with the kings and high visiers of earth
>   who build themselves vast vaults.
> . . . .
> Why give light to a man of grief?
>   Why give life to those bitter of heart,
> who long for a death that never comes . . . ?
> . . . .
> Why make this gift of light to a man who does not see his way,
>   whom God baulks on every side?[15]

The ultimate questions have now been asked and the rest of the drama will convey the implied answers, embedded in symbolic imagery. One might even say that these bitter questions were the contents of the vial poured on Job by Satan. At least these questions are a consequence of Job's being used as a chosen vessel to hold divine contents.

Job has been confronted with the ultimate, metaphysical questions of existence. Once these questions have constellated, the individual must respond in one of three ways. 1) In despair at finding himself

15. Job 3: 3-23, Jerusalem Bible.

an orphan in the cosmos, he may commit suicide either literally or psychologically, for example by succumbing to cynicism. 2) He may find containment in a community or creed that provides an adequate religious myth to silence the questions that have been raised. 3) The third possibility is that a numinous encounter with the Self may occur, through which the individual is granted a direct experience of the archetypal reality that underlies conscious existence. Such an event answers *experientially* the urgent questions which have been raised.

Shall mortal Man be more Just than God? Shall a Man be more Pure than his Maker? Behold he putteth no trust in his Saints & his Angels he chargeth with folly

W Blake invenit & sculp

Then a Spirit passed before my face
the hair of my flesh stood up

London. Published as the Act directs March 8: 1825 by William Blake N 3 Fountain Court. Strand

Proof

Picture 9

Job's comforters are now talking to him. These figures can be best understood as personified images from the personal unconscious encountered in active imagination. Their remarks are a contaminated mixture of several elements of differing value which are characteristic of active imagination and which call for an active, critical attitude on the part of the ego. This picture illustrates a particular speech of Eliphaz:

> Now, I have had a secret revelation,
>   a whisper has come to my ears,
> At the hour when dreams master the mind,
>   and slumber lies heavy on man,
> A shiver of horror ran through me,
>   and my bones quaked with fear.
> A breath slid over my face,
>   the hairs of my body bristled.
> Someone stood there—I could not see his face,
>   but the form remained before me.
>   Silence—and then I heard a Voice,
> "Was ever any man found blameless in the presence of God,
>   or faultless in the presence of his maker?"[16]

This must have been a numinous dream of Job's which is being recalled in his active imagination. It is a kind of dream prelude to the later full encounter with Yahweh.

16. Ibid., 4: 12-17.

But he knoweth the way that I take
when he hath tried me I shall come forth like gold

Have pity upon me! Have pity upon me! O ye my friends
for the hand of God hath touched me

Though he slay me yet will I trust in him

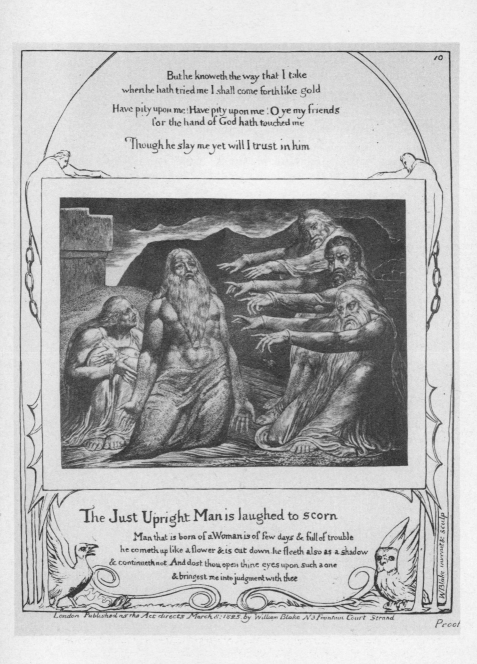

The Just Upright Man is laughed to scorn

Man that is born of a Woman is of few days & full of trouble
he cometh up like a flower & is cut down. he fleeth also as a shadow
& continueth not And dost thou open thine eyes upon such a one
& bringest me into judgment with thee

London Published as the Act directs March 8: 1825. by William Blake N3 Fountain Court Strand

W Blake invent & sculp

Proof

Picture 10

In this picture, Job is the victim of a barrage of accusations from his so-called comforters. Since he is convinced of his innocence and unconscious of his shadow, the personal unconscious compensates by criticizing him.

A good case can be made for the idea that Job is inflated and needs awareness of his shadow as provided by the criticism of his comforters.[17] This type of reductive understanding is suitable for the young and promotes ego development while minimizing the importance of the unconscious. However, it misses the main point of the Book of Job. It is essential that Job *not* succumb to the personalistic interpretations of his counselors. If he were to decide that his misfortunes were all his own fault he would preclude the possibility of a manifestation of the *numinosum*. The ego-vessel would be broken, would lose its integrity, and could have no divine manifestation poured into it. By holding fast to its own experience as an authentic center of being, the Job-ego brings about the visible manifestation of the "other," the transpersonal center.

17. See Edward F. Edinger, *Ego and Archetype: Individuation and the Religious Function of the Psyche* (Baltimore: Pelican Books, 1973), pp. 76ff.

My bones are pierced in me in the
night season & my sinews
take no rest

My skin is black upon me
& my bones are burned
with heat

11

The triumphing of the wicked
is short, the joy of the hypocrite is
but for a moment
Satan himself is transformed into an Angel of Light & his Ministers into Ministers of Righteousness

With Dreams upon my bed thou scarest me & affrightest me
with Visions

Why do you persecute me as God & are not satisfied with my flesh. Oh that my words
were printed in a Book that they were graven with an iron pen & lead in the rock for ever
For I know that my Redeemer liveth & that he shall stand in the latter days upon
the Earth & after my skin destroy thou This body yet in my flesh shall I see God
whom I shall see for Myself and mine eyes shall behold & not Another tho consumed be my wrought Image

Who opposeth & exalteth himself above all that is called God or is Worshipped

W Blake invent & sculp

London Published as the Act directs March 8 1825 by Will Blake N 3 Fountain Court Strand

Proof

Picture 11

This picture illustrates Job's remark,

> If I say, "My bed will comfort me,
>   my couch will soothe my pain,"
> you frighten me with dreams
>   and terrify me with visions.[18]

Yahweh's double nature is here portrayed in frightful fashion. He is entwined by a great snake and a cloven hoof is visible. Yahweh's right hand points to the tablets of the Law and his left hand points to hell which has opened up and threatens to engulf Job. Job here stares into the abyss, the negative *numinosum*. We are reminded of Jung's remark that "the horrified perception of the reality of evil has led to at least as many conversions as the experience of good."[19]

Whereas previously Satan had been associated with fire, now Yahweh himself has taken on that attribute and points to hell as one of his own manifestations. Recall the earlier quotation from *The Marriage of Heaven and Hell* where Blake says that "the Jehovah of the Bible [is] no other than he who dwells in flaming fire." Yahweh and Satan have now become one. As Jung tells us, one aspect of God is "a seething lake of fire."[20] To live by the book protects one from that fire unless or until the satanic eye of Yahweh is activated and sets off another performance of the drama of Job.

---

18. Job 7: 13-14, Jerusalem Bible.
19. Jung, *Psychology and Alchemy*, CW 12, par. 19.
20. Jung, *Answer to Job*, par. 733.

For God speaketh once yea twice & Man perceiveth it not

In a Dream in a Vision of the Night in deep Slumberings upon the bed then he openeth the ears of Man & sealeth their instruction

That he may withdraw Man from his purpose & hide Pride from Man
If there be with him an Interpreter One among a Thousand
then he is gracious unto him & saith Deliver him from going down to the Pit
I have found a Ransom

For his eyes are upon the ways of Man & he observeth all his goings

I am Young & ye are very Old wherefore I was afraid

Lo all these things worketh God oftentimes with Man to bring back his Soul from the pit to be enlightened with the light of the living

Look upon the heavens & behold the clouds which are higher than thou

If thou sinnest what doest thou against him or if thou be righteous what givest thou unto him

WBlake invenit & sculpt

London Published as the Act directs March 8: 1825 by Will Blake N3 Fountain Court Strand

Proof

Here a new man, a fourth one previously unmentioned, enters the picture—Elihu. A change of psychic atmosphere is indicated by the presence of stars for the first time. It is as though Job's encounter with the abyss had caused a change.

The fourth figure signifies the emergence of Job's totality. Elihu is a young man who begins by saying,

> I am still young, and you are old,
>   so I was shy, afraid to tell you what I know.
> I told myself, "Old age should speak,
>   advancing years will utter wisdom!"
> But now I know that it is a breath in man,
>   the inspiration of Shaddai, that gives discernment.[21]

Elihu is the young and fresh aspect of the psyche, the undeveloped function, the child, that which is closest to the unconscious. It is this figure which is the harbinger of the Self. Elihu's remarks present many of the same ideas that Yahweh will soon express more forcefully. Particularly noteworthy are Elihu's statements about dreams:

> God speaks first in one way
>   and then in another, but no one notices.
> He speaks by dreams, and visions that come in the night,
>   when slumber comes on mankind,
>   and men are all asleep in bed.
> Then it is he whispers in the ear of man,
>   or may frighten him with fearful sights
> to turn him away from evil doing
>   and make an end of his pride;
> to save his soul from the pit
>   and his life from the pathway to Sheol.[22]

It is remarkable to discover in this ancient text a statement concerning the compensatory function of dreams.

---

21. Job 32: 6-8, Jerusalem Bible.
22. Ibid., 35: 14-18.

Who is this that darkeneth counsel by words without knowledge

Then the Lord answered Job out of the Whirlwind

Who maketh the Clouds his Chariot & walketh on the Wings of the Wind   the Drops of the Dew

Hath the Rain   a Father & who hath begotten

WBlake invent & sculp

London Published as the Act directs March 8: 1825 by William Blake N 3 Fountain Court Strand

Proof

Picture 13

Now finally the full *numinosum* manifests; Yahweh appears to Job out of the whirlwind.

> Who is this obscuring my designs
> with his empty-headed words?
> Brace yourself like a fighter;
> now it is my turn to ask questions and yours to inform me.
> Where were you when I laid the earth's foundations?
> Tell me, since you are so well informed!
> Who decided the dimensions of it, do you know?
> Or who stretched the measuring line across it?
> What supports its pillars at their bases?
> Who laid its cornerstone
> when all the stars of the morning were singing with joy,
> and the Sons of God in chorus were chanting praise?
> Who pent up the sea behind closed doors
> when it leapt tumultuous out of the womb,
> when I wrapped it in a robe of mist
> and made black clouds its swaddling bands;
> when I marked the bounds it was not to cross
> and made it fast with a bolted gate?
> Come thus far, I said, and no farther:
> here your proud waves shall break.[23]

The distinction between the ego and the Self is here presented with stunning force. Job is discovering the autonomy of the psyche. Wind that blows where it will always carries that symbolism. However, the way Yahweh addresses Job greatly augments the latter's importance. Jung writes,

> Job is challenged as though he himself were a god. But in the contemporary metaphysics there was . . . no other god except Satan . . . . In his stead God must set up his miserable servant as a bugbear whom he has to fight. . . .
>   . . . The conflict becomes acute for Yahweh as a result of a new

23. Ibid., 38: 2-11.

factor . . . . The new factor is something that has never occurred
before in the history of the world, the unheard-of fact that, without
knowing it or wanting it, a mortal man is raised by his moral behaviour
above the stars in heaven, from which position of advantage he can
behold the back of Yahweh, the abysmal world of "shards."[24]

We might ask what does Jung mean by Job's "moral behaviour?"
I think he refers to Job's refusal to accept responsibility for events
that he knows he did not cause. Job's intellectual honesty, his loyalty
to his own perception of reality, his integrity in maintaining the
distinction between subject and object, between man and God—all
these go to make up Job's moral behaviour, which has forced God
to reveal himself.

Job's encounter with Yahweh in the whirlwind taught him a basic
lesson. In his innocence, like orthodox theologians of all creeds,
Job has assumed that God's reality must correspond to his conception
of it. The living experience shatters that assumption.

24. Jung, *Answer to Job,* pars. 594-595.

Canst thou bind the sweet influences of Pleiades or loose the bands of Orion

14

Let there Be

Light

Let there be A

Firmament

Let the Waters be gathered
together into one place

Let the Dry Land
appear

And God made Two Great Lights

Sun

Moon

Let the Waters bring
forth abundantly

Let the Earth bring forth

Cattle & Creeping thing
& Beast

When the morning Stars sang together. & all the
Sons of God shouted for joy

W Blake Invenit & Sc

London. Published as the Act directs March 8. 1825 by Will Blake N 3 Fountain Court Strand.

Proof

Picture 14

The numinous experience continues in a more structured form. At first Yahweh had appeared as an undifferentiated energy-phenomenon, the whirlwind. Now, in this picture, a structured universe is revealed in an image of totality.

In the heavenly realm we see a numerical series of 1, 2, 4, represented by Yahweh as one, Apollo and Artemis as two and the four angels as four. Even more important is the fact that this is an image of creation. In the margin are quotations from the story of creation in Genesis: "Let there Be Light." "Let there be A Firmament." "Let the Waters be gathered together into one place & let the Dry Land appear." "And God made Two Great Lights." "Let the Waters bring forth abundantly." "Let the Earth bring forth Cattle & Creeping thing & beast."

It is most interesting that an image of world-creation should appear at this point. I am reminded of a passage in the alchemical *Emerald Tablet of Hermes*. At the end of the recipe comes the phrase, "Thus the world has been created." The alchemists considered the creation of the Philosophers' Stone, the goal of the opus, as equivalent to the creation of the world. Job's torturous ordeal is analogous to the ordeal imposed on the *prima materia* in the alchemical vessel; in each case, out of the ordeal a world is born.

It is as though Job's encounter with Yahweh in his raw, undifferentiated form were a conception, a process of fertilization that brings about a new creation. The alchemists spoke of the *prima materia* as an *increatum,* matter that had not yet undergone the process of creation.[25] Job's encounter with Yahweh in his uncreated form seems to have the effect of initiating a new creation. This corresponds to the effects we observe when the ego meets the unconscious—the undifferentiated *prima materia* of the psyche. A process of creative differentiation often ensues which amounts to a regeneration of the personality. This happens in the case of Job.

25. Jung, *Psychology and Alchemy*, CW 12, par. 430.

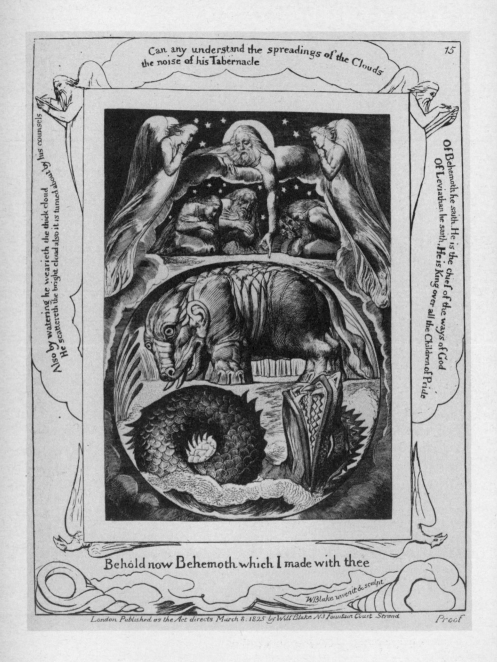

Can any understand the spreadings of the Clouds
the noise of his Tabernacle

Also by watering he wearieth the thick cloud
He scattereth the bright cloud also it is turned about by his counsels

Of Behemoth he saith, He is the chief of the ways of God
Of Leviathan he saith, He is King over all the Children of Pride

Behold now Behemoth which I made with thee

W Blake invenit & sculpt

London Published as the Act directs March 8. 1825 by Will Blake N3 Fountain Court Strand

Proof

Picture 15

Here we have the infernal or chthonic aspects of the *numinosum* as Behemoth and Leviathan. This is the other side of the *numinosum* which we must always remember is a union of opposites.

In the previous picture Job was below, looking up at creation as manifested in the heavens. In this picture he is above, surrounded by stars, looking down at the inhabitants of the abyss. He has temporarily risen above his biological being and is looking down at it. Yahweh is saying,

> Behold Behemoth which I made as I made you.
>
> . . .
>
> Can you draw out Leviathan with a fish hook,
> or press down his tongue with a cord?[26]

Job is being shown the abysmal aspect of God and the depths of his own psyche, which contains devouring monsters remote from human values. Behemoth and Leviathan represent the primordial concupiscence of being. God reveals his own shadow side, and since man participates in God as the ground of his being he must likewise share his darkness. This illustrates the fact that our existence is based on protoplasm—greedy, lusting, devouring matter.

Jung writes:

> Formerly [Job] was naïve, dreaming perhaps of a "good" God, or of a benevolent ruler and just judge. He had imagined that a "covenant" was a legal matter and that anyone who was party to a contract could insist on his rights as agreed; that God would be faithful and true or at least just, and, as one could assume from the Ten Commandments, would have some recognition of ethical values or at least feel committed to his own legal standpoint. But, to his horror, he has discovered that Yahweh is not human but, in certain respects, less than human, that he is just what Yahweh himself says of Leviathan (the crocodile):
>
>> He beholds everything that is high:
>> He is king over all proud beasts. [Job 41:25; Zurich Bible]

26. Job 40:15, 41:1, Revised Standard Version.

Unconsciousness has an animal nature. Like all old gods Yahweh has his animal symbolism with its unmistakable borrowings from the much older theriomorphic gods of Egypt, especially Horus and his four sons. Of the four animals of Yahweh only one has a human face. That is probably Satan, the god-father of man as a spiritual being. Ezekiel's vision attributes three-fourths animal nature and only one-fourth human nature to the animal deity, while the upper deity, the one above the "sapphire throne," merely had the "likeness" of a man. This symbolism explains Yahweh's behaviour, which, from the human point of view, is so intolerable: it is the behaviour of an unconscious being who cannot be judged morally. Yahweh is a *phenomenon* and, as Job says, "not a man."[27]

27. Jung, *Answer to Job,* pars. 599-600.

16

Hell is naked before him & Destruction has no covering

Canst thou find out the Almighty to perfection

Canst thou by searching find out God

The Accuser of our Brethren is Cast down
which accused them before our God day & night

It is higher than Heaven what canst thou do

It is deeper than Hell what canst thou know

The Prince of this World shall be cast out

Even the Devils are Subject to Us thro thy Name. Jesus said unto them. I saw Satan as lightning fall from Heaven

Thou hast fulfilled the Judgment of the Wicked

God hath chosen the foolish things of the World to confound the wise
And God hath chosen the weak things of the World to confound the things that are mighty

W Blake inv & sculp

London. Published as the Act directs March 8: 1825 by J Linnell Cirencester Place Fitzroy Square

Picture 16

This picture comes not from the Book of Job but rather illustrates a remark of Jesus: "I watched Satan fall like lightning from heaven."[28]

It is very interesting that Blake should follow his portrayal of the encounter between Job and Yahweh with a picture of Satan's being cast out of heaven as witnessed by Jesus. According to Jung, Yahweh became aware of his lack of moral differentiation through meeting Job and therefore had to give satisfaction to Job by incarnating in Christ.[29] This involved at the same time a decisive separation of Yahweh and Satan, represented by Satan's being cast out of heaven. Jung notes that Satan had little effect on the events of the Incarnation and continues:

> His comparative ineffectiveness can be explained on the one hand by the careful preparations for the divine birth, and on the other hand by a curious metaphysical phenomenon which Christ witnessed: he saw Satan fall like lightning from heaven. In this vision a metaphysical event has become temporal; it indicates the historic and—so far as we know—final separation of Yahweh from his dark son. Satan is banished from heaven and no longer has any opportunity to inveigle his father into dubious undertakings. This event may well explain why he plays such an inferior role wherever he appears in the history of the Incarnation. His role here is in no way comparable to his former confidential relationship to Yahweh. He has obviously forfeited the paternal affection and been exiled. The punishment which we missed in the story of Job has at last caught up with him, though in a strangely limited form. Although he is banished from the heavenly court he has kept his dominion over the sublunary world. He is not cast directly into hell, but upon earth. Only at the end of time shall he be locked up and made permanently ineffective.[30]

Blake does not follow the New Testament account precisely. In this picture Satan is being cast into hell, indicating that, according

28. Luke 10:18, Jerusalem Bible.
29. Jung, *Answer to Job*, par. 642.
30. Ibid., par. 650.

to the Christian framework, we are seeing an eschatological event at the end of time. Psychologically, it indicates a decisive separation of the opposites. A division is occurring between Yahweh and Satan and between Job and his shadow figures. A full synthesis has not been achieved but rather a higher level of differentiation.

He bringeth down to   he shall appear we shall be like him for we shall   the Grave & bringeth up   17

We know that when

When I behold the Heavens the work of thy hands the Moon & Stars which thou hast ordained. then I say What is Man that thou art mindful of him? & the Son of Man that thou visitest him

I have heard thee with the hearing of the Ear but now my Eye seeth thee.

He that hath seen me

If you had known me ye would have known my Father also and from henceforth ye know him & have seen him

Believe me that I am in the Father & that Father in me the that loveth me shall be loved of my Father & I for I shall dwell in & words shall be with you

hath seen my Father also
I & my Father are One

At that day ye shall know that I am in my Father & you in me & I in you
If ye loved me ye would rejoice because I said I go unto the Father

He that loveth me shall be loved of my Father & I will love him & manifest myself unto him And my Father will come unto him & make our abode with him

And the Father shall give you another Comforter that he may abide with you for ever Even the Spirit of Truth whom the World cannot receive

WBlake

inv & sculp

London Published as the Act directs March 8 1825 by William Blake N° 3 Fountain Court Strand

Proof

Picture 17

Job's relation to Yahweh has now been healed. The ego's rapport with the Self—the ego-Self axis—has been restored. In the lower margin Blake quotes the saying of Christ in John 14:20. "At that day ye shall know that I am in my Father & you in me & I in you." This quotation states explicitly that Job is reconciled to Yahweh through Christ, the same point that Jung makes in *Answer to Job*. In other words, Yahweh's encounter with Job has required him, Yahweh, to undergo the Christian transformation. This will be the new world that Blake portrayed in Picture 14.

Although Job is reinstated in Yahweh's good graces, all elements of the personality do not share in the restoration. Job's friends have their backs to Yahweh and seem to be banished from his blessing. This indicates that the shadow remains in repression and full integration remains for the future. The image of the light and dark sides' having their backs to each other is reminiscent of Jacob Böhme's split mandala (see next page), which Jung refers to in "A Study in the Process of Individuation."[31]

Both Böhme and Blake were extreme introverted intuitive types who were one-sidedly spiritual with very little relation to the reality of the senses. Blake's lack of integration of the earthy, shadow side probably accounts for the lack of a fully developed mandala in this series. Also he led a life compensatory to his time which was extraverted, rational and sensation-reality oriented. The collective world-view of Blake's time would therefore have been his shadow, personified by Newton and Bacon.

31. Jung, *The Archetypes and the Collective Unconscious*, CW 9, I, par. 534.

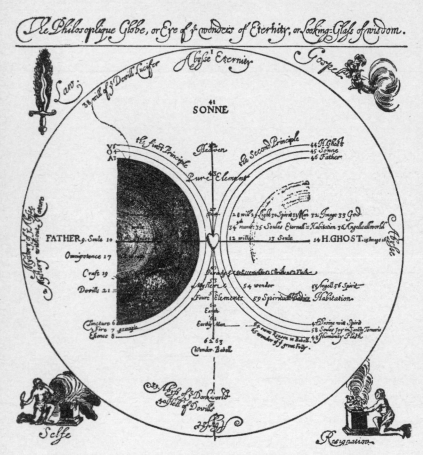

Split mandala from Jacob Böhme's *XL Questions concerning the Soule* (1620)

18

Also the Lord accepted Job

And my Servant Job shall pray for you

And the Lord turned the captivity of Job when he prayed for his Friends

W Blake inv & sculp

London Published as the Act directs March 8 1825 by Will Blake N 3 Fountain Court Strand

Proof

Picture 18

This picture illustrates the attitude brought about by Job's encounter with Yahweh. He is facing inward and offering a burnt sacrifice to Yahweh. What is pictured here is thus a sacrificial attitude. Jung's subtle and profound interpretation of this, expressed throughout *Answer to Job,* is paraphrased by Rivkah Kluger:

> In his great final speech God reveals himself to Job in all his frightfulness. It is as if he said to Job: "Look, that's what I am like. That is why I treated you like this." Through the suffering which he inflicted upon Job out of his own nature, God has come to this self-knowledge and admits, as it were, this knowledge of his frightfulness to Job. And that is what redeems the man Job. This is really the solution of the enigma of Job, that is, a true justification for Job's fate, which, without this background, would, in its cruelty and injustice, remain an open problem. Job appears here clearly as a sacrifice, but also as the carrier of the divine fate, and that gives meaning to his suffering and liberation to his soul.[32]

Job is a sacrifice for Yahweh's developing consciousness. At first he is an involuntary victim. After the theophany, when he sees the reality of Yahweh with his own eyes, he takes on the attitude of voluntary sacrifice:

> I had heard of thee by the hearing of the ear,
>   but now my eye sees thee;
> therefore I despise myself,
>   and repent in dust and ashes.[33]

Job's comforters are no longer separated from him. The sacrificial attitude brings unity to the personality as ego, shadow figures and wife-anima turn toward the center which they serve and which unites them.

32. Rivkah Kluger, *Satan in the Old Testament* (Evanston: Northwestern University Press, 1967), p. 129.
33. Job 42: 5-6, Revised Standard Version.

19

The Lord maketh Poor & maketh Rich

He bringeth Low & Lifteth Up

who provideth for the
Raven his Food
When his young ones cry unto God

Every one also gave him a piece of Money

Who remembered us in our low estate
For his Mercy endureth for ever

W Blake inv & sculp

London, Published as the Act directs March 8, 1825, by William Blake N 3 Fountain Court, Strand

Proof

Picture 19

The Book of Job concludes with these words:

> Yahweh restored Job's fortunes, because he had prayed for his friends. More than that, Yahweh gave him double what he had before. And all his brothers and all his sisters and all his friends of former times came to see him and sat down at table with him. They showed him every sympathy, and comforted him for all the evils Yahweh had inflicted on him. Each of them gave him a silver coin, and each a gold ring. Yahweh blessed Job's new fortune even more than his first one. He came to own fourteen thousand sheep, six thousand camels, a thousand yoke of oxen and a thousand she-donkeys. He had seven sons and three daughters: his first daughter he called "Turtledove," the second "Cassia" and the third "Mascara." Throughout the land there were no women as beautiful as the daughters of Job. And their father gave them inheritance rights like their brothers.
>
> After his trials, Job lived on until he was a hundred and forty years old, and saw his children and his children's children up to the fourth generation. Then Job died, an old man and full of days.[34]

The picture shows his family and friends each bringing him money and a gold ring. This expresses the unification of the personality. Money signifies libido and this is now becoming available to the ego from all the various aspects of the psyche. A ring signifies unity, wholeness and the marriage pledge—that is, it is an emblem of the *coniunctio*—the union of opposites in the psyche. A field of ripe grain is in the background. The fruits of the ordeal are now to be harvested. Job's fortunes have not only been restored but there has also been an enlargement of the personality as a result of the encounter with the *numinosum*. As Jung puts it, "the widening of consciousness is at first upheaval and darkness, then a broadening out of man to the whole man."[35]

34. Job 42: 10-17, Jerusalem Bible.
35. Jung, *Mysterium Coniunctionis,* CW 14, par. 209.

20

How precious are thy thoughts
unto me O God
how great is the sum of them

There were not found. Women fair as the Daughters of Job

in all the Land & their Father gave them Inheritance

among their Brethren

If I ascend up into Heaven thou art there
If I make my bed in Hell behold Thou
art there

W Blake invenit & sc

London. Published as the Act directs March 8: 1825 by William Blake N° 3 Fountain Court Strand.

Proof

Picture 20

Here Job is instructing his daughters. Scenes of his encounter with Yahweh are in the background. It is interesting that the feminine factor is given special prominence at the end. The three daughters are named, mentioned as particularly beautiful and given equal inheritance rights—something very unusual for the time. Clearly, the one-sided patriarchy of the "book" has been superseded as a consequence of Job's ordeal and the feminine principle has come into proper prominence. In the picture of sacrifice, Job faced inward; now he faces outward, using the experience of his ordeal as the basis for instruction of others.

Job's newly established relation to his daughters corresponds to what Jung says happened to Yahweh after his encounter with Job. He remembered his playmate Sophia, "a feminine being who is no less agreeable to him than to man, a friend and playmate from the beginning of the world."[36] Yahweh had treated Job in a shockingly unrelated way. His feminine side had been missing and must be recovered, as it is here with Job.

36. Jung, *Answer to Job*, par. 617. See also Proverbs 8, where Wisdom (Sophia) speaks: "Then I was by him, as one brought up with him."

21

Great & Marvellous are thy Works Lord God Almughty

Just & True are thy Ways O thou King of Saints

So the Lord blessed the latter end of Job
more than the beginning

After this Job lived
an hundred & forty years
& saw his Sons & his
Sons Sons

even four Generations
So Job died
being old
& full of days

In burnt Offerings for Sin

thou hast had no Pleasure

W Blake inv & sculp

London Published as the Act directs March 8:1825 by William Blake Fountain Court Strand

Proof.

Picture 21

The final picture shows Job, his wife and new family gathered around the tree of life once again under new and different circumstances. It is dawn, the sun is rising on the right. On the left is the moon in its waxing phase. Previously all had been sitting, now they are standing. The animals are awake instead of asleep and the musical instruments are being played. A rejuvenation of life is here represented following the *nekyia,* the dark night of Job's encounter with the unconscious. He is now in a conscious relation to the reality of the Self (Yahweh), to instinctual energies (the animals), and to the spiritual, creative and feeling factors (the musical instruments). And most important of all, Job is now aware of being "the carrier of the divine fate and that gives meaning to his suffering and liberation to his soul."[37]

As in the first picture, here again is the flaming sacrificial altar; again the picture is framed by the cloud of smoke rising from that altar and again a tentlike form surrounds them all, as though the picture were a window looking into the Holy Tabernacle.

The lesson of the Job story for modern man is described by Jung in his letter of June 30, 1956, to Elined Kotschnig, who had asked for an answer to "the problem of an unconscious, ignorant creator-god."[38] Jung replies:

> We have become participants of the divine life and we have to assume a new responsibility, viz. the continuation of the divine self-realization, which expresses itself in the task of our individuation. Individuation does not only mean that man has become truly human as distinct from animal, but that he is to become partially divine as well. This means practically that he becomes adult, responsible for his existence, knowing that he does not only depend on God but that God also depends on man. Man's relation to God probably has to undergo a certain important change: Instead of the propitiating praise to an

37. Kluger, *Satan in the Old Testament,* p. 129.
38. *C.G. Jung Letters,* ed. G. Adler and A. Jaffé, Bollingen Series XCV (Princeton: Princeton University Press, 1975), vol. 2, p. 312n.

74

unpredictable king or the child's prayer to a loving father, the responsible living and fulfilling of the divine will in us will be our form of worship of and commerce with God. His goodness means grace and light and His dark side the terrible temptation of power.[39]

Although the divine incarnation is a cosmic and absolute event, it only manifests empirically in those relatively few individuals capable of enough consciousness to make ethical decisions, i.e., to decide for the Good. Therefore God can be called good only inasmuch as He is able to manifest His goodness in individuals. His moral quality depends upon individuals. That is why He incarnates. Individuation and individual existence are indispensable for the transformation of God the Creator.[40]

The mythological phoenix, symbol of transformation
(Boschius, *Symbolographia,* 1702)

39. Ibid., p. 316.
40. Ibid., p. 314.

Publisher's Note

Encounter with the Self is a companion volume to Edward F. Edinger's *The Creation of Consciousness: Jung's Myth for Modern Man,* title number 14 in the series published by Inner City Books (see descriptions on the following pages).

The Creation of Consciousness is comprised of four long essays. Using religious and alchemical texts, mythology, modern dreams and the concepts of depth psychology, the author proposes nothing less than a new world-view—a creative collaboration between the scientific pursuit of knowledge and the religious search for meaning.

"Religion is based on Eros, science on Logos," writes Dr. Edinger. "Religion sought linkage with God, science sought knowledge. The age now dawning seeks *linked knowledge.*"

The first essay traces the outlines of a "new myth" emerging from the life and work of C.G. Jung—not another religion in competition with all the others, but rather a psychological standpoint from which to understand and verify the essential meaning of every religion.

The second essay discusses the purpose of human life and what it means to be conscious, "knowing together with an other." In religious terms the "other" is God; psychologically it is the Self, archetype of wholeness and the regulating center of the psyche.

The third essay examines at length the implications of Jung's masterwork, *Answer to Job,* in which Jung demonstrates that God needs man in order to become conscious of His dark side. Depth psychology, the "new dispensation," finds man's relation to what has traditionally been called God in the individual's experience of the unconscious.

The final essay explores Jung's belief that "God's moral quality depends on individuals," which translates psychologically into the pressing need for man to become more conscious of his own dark, destructive side as well as his creative potential.

The Creation of Consciousness is an important book, written in the shadow of ominous global forces. Its basic focus on the quality and meaning of individual human lives reflects an underlying concern for the continuation on earth of any life at all.

Studies in Jungian Psychology
by Jungian Analysts

LIMITED EDITION PAPERBACKS

Prices quoted are in U.S. dollars (except for Canadian orders)

1. The Secret Raven: Conflict and Transformation.
Daryl Sharp (Toronto). ISBN 0-919123-00-7. 128 pages. $10

A concise introduction to the application of Jungian psychology. Focuses on the creative personality—and the life and dreams of the writer Franz Kafka —but the psychology is relevant to anyone who has experienced a conflict between the spiritual life and sex, or between inner and outer reality. (Knowledge of Kafka is not necessary.) Illustrated. Bibliography.

2. The Psychological Meaning of Redemption Motifs in Fairytales.
Marie-Louise von Franz (Zurich). ISBN 0-919123-01-5. 128 pages. $10

A unique account of the significance of fairytales for an understanding of the process of individuation, especially in terms of integrating animal nature and human nature. Particularly helpful for its symbolic, nonlinear approach to the meaning of typical dream motifs (bathing, beating, clothes, animals, etc.), and its clear description of complexes and projection.

3. On Divination and Synchronicity: Psychology of Meaningful Chance.
Marie-Louise von Franz (Zurich). ISBN 0-919123-02-3. 128 pages. $10

A penetrating study of the meaning of the irrational. Examines time, number, and methods of divining fate such as the I Ching, astrology, Tarot, palmistry, random patterns, etc. Explains Jung's ideas on archetypes, projection, psychic energy and synchronicity, contrasting Western scientific attitudes with those of the Chinese and so-called primitives. Illustrated.

4. The Owl Was a Baker's Daughter: Obesity, Anorexia Nervosa, and the Repressed Feminine.
Marion Woodman (Toronto). ISBN 0-919123-03-1. 144 pages. $10

A pioneer work in feminine psychology, with particular attention to the body as mirror of the psyche in eating disorders and weight disturbances. Explores the personal and cultural loss—and potential rediscovery—of the feminine principle, through Jung's Association Experiment, case studies, dreams, Christianity and mythology. Illustrated. Glossary. Bibliography.

5. Alchemy: An Introduction to the Symbolism and the Psychology.
Marie-Louise von Franz (Zurich). ISBN 0-919123-04-X. 288 pages. $16

A lucid and practical guide to what the alchemists were really looking for— emotional balance and wholeness. Completely demystifies the subject. An important work, invaluable for an understanding of images and motifs in modern dreams and drawings, and indispensable for anyone interested in relationships and communication between the sexes. 84 Illustrations.

6. Descent to the Goddess: A Way of Initiation for Women.
Sylvia Brinton Perera (New York). ISBN 0-919123-05-8. 112 pages. $10

A timely and provocative study of women's freedom and the need for an inner, female authority in a masculine-oriented society. Based on the Sumerian goddess Inanna-Ishtar's journey to the underworld, her transformation through contact with her dark "sister" Ereshkigal, and her return. Rich in insights from dreams, mythology and analysis. Glossary. Bibliography.

7. The Psyche as Sacrament: C.G. Jung and Paul Tillich.
John P. Dourley (Ottawa). ISBN 0-919123-06-6. 128 pages. $10

An illuminating, comparative study showing with great clarity that in the depths of the soul the psychological task and the religious task are one. With a dual perspective, the author—Jungian analyst and Catholic priest—examines the deeper meaning, for Christian and non-Christian alike, of God, Christ, the Spirit, the Trinity, morality and the religious life. Glossary.

8. Border Crossings: Carlos Castaneda's Path of Knowledge.
Donald Lee Williams (Boulder). ISBN 0-919123-07-4. 160 pages. $12

The first thorough psychological examination of the popular don Juan novels. Using dreams, fairytales, and mythic and cultural parallels, the author brings Castaneda's spiritual journey down to earth, in terms of everyone's search for self-realization. Special attention to the psychology of women. (Familiarity with the novels is not necessary.) Glossary.

9. Narcissism and Character Transformation: The Psychology of Narcissistic Character Disorders.
Nathan Schwartz-Salant (New York). ISBN 0-919123-08-2. 192 pp. $13

An incisive and comprehensive analysis of narcissism: what it looks like, what it means and how to deal with it. Shows how an understanding of the archetypal patterns that underlie the individual, clinical symptoms of narcissism can point the way to a healthy restructuring of the personality. Draws upon a variety of psychoanalytic points of view (Jungian, Freudian, Kohutian, Kleinian, etc.). Illustrated. Glossary. Bibliography.

10. Rape and Ritual: A Psychological Study.
Bradley A. Te Paske (Minneapolis). ISBN 0-919123-09-0. 160 pp. $12

An absorbing combination of theory, clinical material, dreams and mythology, penetrating far beyond the actual deed to the impersonal, archetypal background of sexual assault. Special attention to male ambivalence toward women and the psychological significance of rape dreams and fantasies. Illustrated. Glossary. Bibliography.

11. Alcoholism and Women: The Background and the Psychology.
Jan Bauer (Zurich). ISBN 0-919123-10-4. 144 pages. $12

A major contribution to an understanding of alcoholism, particularly in women. Compares and contrasts medical and psychological models, illustrates the relative merits of Alcoholics Anonymous and individual therapy, and presents new ways of looking at the problem based on case material, dreams and archetypal patterns. Glossary. Bibliography.

12. Addiction to Perfection: The Still Unravished Bride.
Marion Woodman (Toronto). ISBN 0-919123-11-2. 208 pages. $12

A powerful and authoritative look at the psychology and attitudes of modern woman, expanding on the themes introduced in *The Owl Was a Baker's Daughter*. Explores the nature of the feminine through case material, dreams and mythology, in food rituals, rape symbolism, perfectionism, imagery in the body, sexuality and creativity. Illustrated.

13. Jungian Dream Interpretation: A Handbook of Theory and Practice.
James A. Hall, M.D. (Dallas). ISBN 0-919123-12-0. 128 pages. $12

A comprehensive and practical guide to an understanding of dreams in light of the basic concepts of Jungian psychology. Jung's model of the psyche is described and discussed, with many clinical examples. Particular attention to common dream motifs, and how dreams are related to the stage of life and individuation process of the dreamer. Glossary.

14. The Creation of Consciousness: Jung's Myth for Modern Man.
Edward F. Edinger, M.D. (Los Angeles). ISBN 0-919123-13-9. 128 pp. $12
An important new book by the author of *Ego and Archetype*. Explores the significance of Jung's work, the meaning of human life and the pressing need for humanity to become conscious of its dark, destructive side. Illustrated.

15. The Analytic Encounter: Transference and Human Relationship.
Mario Jacoby (Zurich). ISBN 0-919123-14-7. 128 pp. $12
A sensitive study illustrating the difference between relationships based on projection and those characterized by psychological objectivity and mutual respect. Shows how complexes manifest in dreams and emotional reactions.

16. Change of Life: Dreams and the Menopause.
Ann Mankowitz (Santa Fe). ISBN 0-919123-15-5. 128 pp. $12
A moving account of a menopausal woman's Jungian analysis, revealing this crucial period as a time of rebirth – a rare opportunity for psychological integration, increased strength and specifically feminine wisdom.

17. The Illness That We Are: A Jungian Critique of Christianity.
John P. Dourley (Ottawa). ISBN 0-919123-16-3. 128 pp. $12
A radical study by Catholic priest and analyst, exploring Jung's views that the Gnostic, mystical and alchemical traditions contain the necessary compensation for the essentially masculine ideals of Christianity.

18. Hags and Heroes: A Feminist Approach to Jungian Psychotherapy with Couples. ISBN 0-919123-17-1. 192 pp. $14
Polly Young-Eisendrath (Philadelphia)
A highly original integration of feminist views with the concepts of Jung and Harry Stack Sullivan. Detailed strategies and techniques; emphasis on revaluing the feminine and re-assessing the nature of female authority.

19. Cultural Attitudes in Psychological Perspective.   128 pp. $12
Joseph L. Henderson, M.D. (San Francisco). ISBN 0-919123-18-X.
A thoughtful new work by the co-author of *Man and His Symbols*. Examines the nature and value of social, religious, aesthetic and philosophic attitudes, showing how the concepts of analytical psychology can give depth and substance to an individual *Weltanschauung*. Illustrated.

20. The Vertical Labyrinth: Individuation in Jungian Psychology.
Aldo Carotenuto (Rome). ISBN 0-919123-19-8. 144 pp. $12
A guided journey through the analytic process, following the dreams of one man who over a lengthy period of analysis finds new life and inner purpose; an individual journey that yet echoes the universal themes of humanity.

21. The Pregnant Virgin: A Process of Psychological Transformation.   Marion Woodman (Toronto). ISBN 0-919123-20-1. 208 pp. $15
A major new work about the struggle to become conscious of our own unique truth and inner potential. Explores the wisdom of the body, relationships, dreams, initiation rituals, addictions (food, drugs, work, etc.). Illustrated.

Add $1 per book (bookpost) or $3 per book (airmail)

INNER CITY BOOKS
Box 1271, Station Q, Toronto, Canada M4T 2P4   (416) 927-0355

ORDER FORM
Please detach and fill out both sides

Prices quoted are in $U.S. (except for Cdn orders)

Title	Price	Copies	Amount
1. Raven	$10	_____	_____
2. Redemption	$10	_____	_____
3. Divination	$10	_____	_____
4. The Owl	$10	_____	_____
5. Alchemy	$16	_____	_____
6. Descent	$10	_____	_____
7. Psyche	$10	_____	_____
8. Border	$12	_____	_____
9. Narcissism	$13	_____	_____
10. Rape	$12	_____	_____
11. Alcoholism	$12	_____	_____
12. Addiction	$12	_____	_____
13. Dream	$12	_____	_____
14. Creation	$12	_____	_____
15. Encounter	$12	_____	_____
16. Change	$12	_____	_____
17. Illness	$12	_____	_____
18. Hags	$14	_____	_____
19. Culture	$12	_____	_____
20. Labyrinth	$12	_____	_____
21. Virgin	$15	_____	_____
22. Self	$10	_____	_____

Subtotal: _____

Plus Postage/Handling: _____
($1 per book or $3 per book airmail)

TOTAL: _____

Orders from outside Canada pay in $U.S.
Please make check or money order (no credit cards)
payable to INNER CITY BOOKS

INNER CITY BOOKS
Box 1271, Station Q
Toronto, Canada M4T 2P4

Check or Money Order enclosed for —————

Please send books to:

NAME: —————

ADDRESS: —————

————— Zip or Postal Code: —————

Please send ————— (quantity) Catalogues/Order Forms to me ————— and ————— to:

NAME: —————

ADDRESS: —————

————— Zip or Postal Code: —————

REMARKS